Good Science—*That's Easy to Teach*

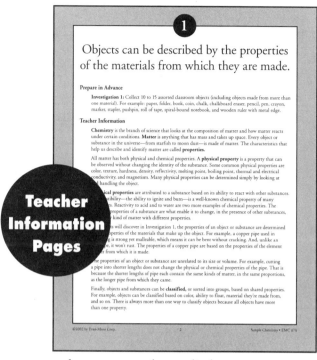

- the concept to be studied
- items to obtain or prepare in advance
- background information

- reproduce or make into transparency

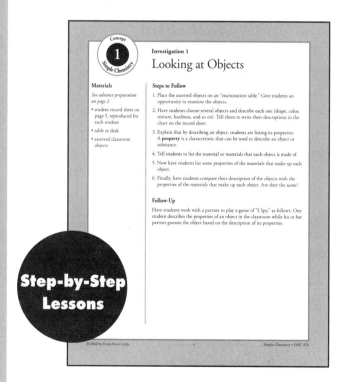

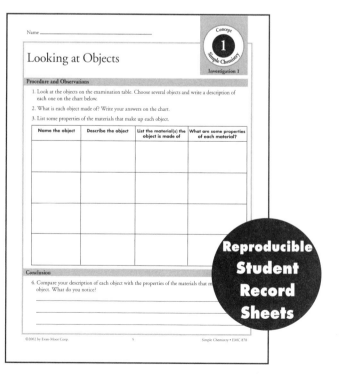

Objects can be described by the properties of the materials from which they are made.

Prepare in Advance

Investigation 1: Collect 10 to 15 assorted classroom objects (including objects made from more than one material). For example: paper, folder, book, coin, chalk, chalkboard eraser, pencil, pen, crayon, marker, stapler, pushpin, roll of tape, spiral-bound notebook, and wooden ruler with metal edge.

Teacher Information

Chemistry is the branch of science that looks at the composition of matter and how matter reacts under certain conditions. **Matter** is anything that has mass and takes up space. Every object or substance in the universe—from starfish to moon dust—is made of matter. The characteristics that help us describe and identify matter are called **properties.**

All matter has both physical and chemical properties. A **physical property** is a property that can be observed without changing the identity of the substance. Some common physical properties are color, texture, hardness, density, reflectivity, melting point, boiling point, thermal and electrical conductivity, and magnetism. Many physical properties can be determined simply by looking at and handling the object.

Chemical properties are attributed to a substance based on its ability to react with other substances. Combustibility—the ability to ignite and burn—is a well-known chemical property of many substances. Reactivity to acid and to water are two more examples of chemical properties. The chemical properties of a substance are what enable it to change, in the presence of other substances, into a new kind of matter with different properties.

As students will discover in Investigation 1, the properties of an object or substance are determined by the properties of the materials that make up the object. For example, a copper pipe used in plumbing is strong yet malleable, which means it can be bent without cracking. And, unlike an iron pipe, it won't rust. The properties of a copper pipe are based on the properties of the element copper, from which it is made.

The properties of an object or substance are unrelated to its size or volume. For example, cutting a pipe into shorter lengths does not change the physical or chemical properties of the pipe. That is because the shorter lengths of pipe each contain the same kinds of matter, in the same proportions, as the longer pipe from which they came.

Finally, objects and substances can be **classified,** or sorted into groups, based on shared properties. For example, objects can be classified based on color, their ability to float, the material they're made from, and so on. There is always more than one way to classify objects because all objects have more than one property.

Classification

Green Things	Bumpy Things	Four-legged Things	Slippery Things	Pocket-size Things
leaf bread mold frog	road gourd frog	table dog frog	soap oil frog	watch baseball card frog

Concept 1 — Simple Chemistry

Investigation 1

Looking at Objects

Materials

See advance preparation on page 2.

- student record sheet on page 5, reproduced for each student
- table or desk
- assorted classroom objects

Steps to Follow

1. Place the assorted objects on an "examination table." Give students an opportunity to examine the objects.

2. Have students choose several objects and describe each one (shape, color, texture, hardness, and so on). Tell them to write their descriptions on the chart on the record sheet.

3. Explain that by describing an object, students are listing its properties. A **property** is a characteristic that can be used to describe an object or substance.

4. Tell students to list the material or materials that each object is made of.

5. Now have students list some properties of the materials that make up each object.

6. Finally, have students compare their description of the objects with the properties of the materials that make up each object. Are they the same?

Follow-Up

Have students work with a partner to play a game of "I Spy," as follows: One student describes the properties of an object in the classroom while his or her partner guesses the object based on the description of its properties.

Concept

1

Simple Chemistry

Investigation 1

Looking at Objects

Procedure and Observations

1. Look at the objects on the examination table. Choose several objects and write a description of each one on the chart below.

2. What is each object made of? Write your answers on the chart.

3. List some properties of the materials that make up each object.

Name the object	Describe the object	List the material(s) the object is made of	What are some properties of each material?

Conclusion

4. Compare your description of each object with the properties of the materials that make up the object. What do you notice?

_____

_____

_____

Investigation 2

Classifying Objects

Materials

- student record sheet on page 7, reproduced for each student

- overhead transparency of *Classification* on page 3

- assorted materials (the same as those used in Investigation 1)

Steps to Follow

1. Give students an opportunity to reexamine the objects they looked at in Investigation 1. Tell students that objects can be **classified,** or sorted into groups, by their properties.

2. Using the *Classification* transparency, go over the descriptions and classification groups with students in order to familiarize them with the process.

3. Have students classify the objects from Investigation 1 according to a given property—for example, their shape, the material they're made from, and so on. Tell students to record their classification groups on the chart on their record sheets.

4. When students have finished, ask several volunteers to share their classification system with the class. Discuss the fact that several correct classification groups are acceptable.

5. Now have students reclassify the objects using a different property. Again have them use the charts to record their classification schemes.

Follow-Up

Ask students to list some of the ways objects are sorted and classified in their household—for example, forks, knives, and spoons in the silverware drawer; white and colored laundry washed separately; and so on.

Name _____

Classifying Objects

Procedure and Observations

1. Examine the objects from Investigation 1 again. Do any of the objects share certain properties with other objects? Give an example.

    _____

2. Choose a property. Then classify the objects based on that property. For example, objects classified by the property "color" could be divided into groups of white, black, silver, and so on. Use the chart below to classify the objects any way you like. Add more groups if you need to.

Property: _____			
Group 1:	**Group 2:**	**Group 3:**	**Group 4:**

3. Now choose a different property and reclassify the objects.

Property: _____			
Group 1:	**Group 2:**	**Group 3:**	**Group 4:**

Conclusion

4. Why is it possible to classify a group of objects in more than one way?

    _____

    _____

Substances can exist in different states—solid, liquid, or gas.

Teacher Information

One important property of matter is its physical form, or state. There are three main **states of matter:** solid, liquid, and gas. Most substances can exist in all three states, although different substances exist in different states at room temperature.

Substances in a **solid** state have a clearly defined shape and a fixed volume. (**Volume** is the amount of space a substance takes up.) Their shape and volume do not change when they are moved from one place to another.

Substances in a **liquid** state do not have a defined shape but instead assume the shape of the container they are poured into (or form a puddle if poured on a flat surface). However, the volume of a liquid remains the same regardless of the container it is in.

Substances that do not have a defined shape or volume are called gases. A **gas** will take the shape of whatever container it is in. It will also spread out to fill any size container. As a result, the volume of gas changes as the size of the container changes.

The state of a substance depends on the motion of the particles that make up the substance. These particles, called **atoms** and **molecules,** are constantly moving and bumping into each other. In a solid, the particles vibrate in place while remaining "locked" together, which is why a solid retains its shape. In a liquid, the particles roll around each other but still remain in contact. That's what causes a liquid to flow and to puddle. In a gas, the particles move freely and in straight lines until they bump into other particles. That's why a gas will spread out indefinitely.

A substance changes state when the speed of its particles is increased or decreased. Heating or cooling a substance is one way to speed up or slow down the motion of the particles. Heating a solid causes it to **melt** (change from a solid to a liquid) by increasing the speed of its particles so that they are able to overcome the attraction that holds them together. Heating a liquid causes it to **vaporize** or **evaporate** (change from a liquid to a gas) in the same way.

Cooling a vapor causes it to **condense** (change from a gas to a liquid) by slowing down the particles so that they cannot overcome the attraction between them. This causes them to clump together, forming a liquid. The same process is at work during **freezing** (changing from a liquid to a solid), except that the particles slow down to the point where they "lock" together, forming a solid.

States of Matter

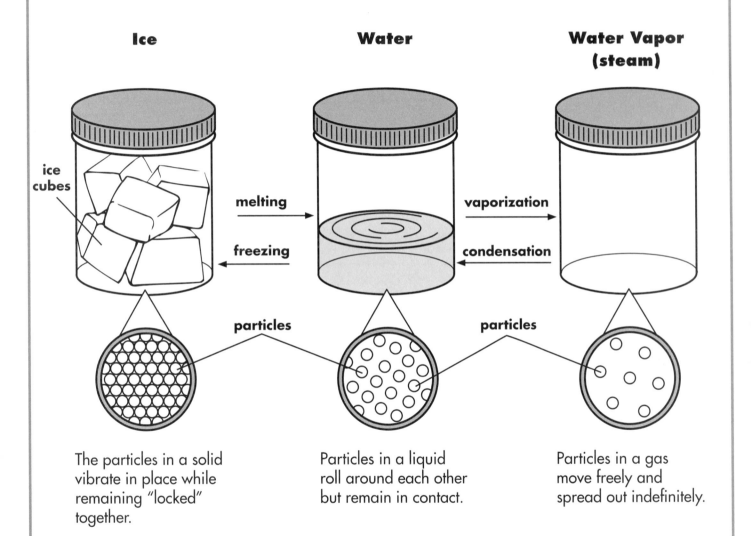

Ice

Water

Water Vapor (steam)

ice cubes

melting

freezing

vaporization

condensation

particles

particles

The particles in a solid vibrate in place while remaining "locked" together.

Particles in a liquid roll around each other but remain in contact.

Particles in a gas move freely and spread out indefinitely.

Investigation 1

What Is a Solid?

Materials

- student record sheet on page 11, reproduced for each student
- cube-shaped wooden blocks
- metric rulers
- glass jars (large enough to hold a block)

Steps to Follow

1. Divide students into small groups. Give each group a wooden block to examine.

2. Ask students what shape the block is. Have them record their observations on their record sheets.

3. Have students find the volume of the block by measuring and then multiplying the length, width, and height of the block. (If the block is 5 cm on one side, its volume will be 125 cm^3.)

4. Tell students that **volume** is the amount of space an object or substance takes up. The volume of the block is measured in units called cubic centimeters (cm^3).

5. Ask students to predict what will happen to the shape and volume of the block when it is placed in a container.

6. Tell students to place the block in the jar and observe any changes to the block's shape and volume. Have them record their observations.

7. Explain that the wooden block is a solid. A **solid** is an object or substance whose shape and volume do not change when it is moved from one place to another. Solid is one of the **states of matter.**

Follow-Up

An object does not have to feel hard like a wooden block in order to be a solid. Have students examine some solids that are soft to the touch, such as a pillow, a marshmallow, a feather, an article of clothing, a sponge, a rubber ball, and so on. What makes each of these objects a solid?

Name _____

What Is a Solid?

Procedure and Observations

1. Look at the wooden block. What shape is it?

   _____

2. Measure the length, width, and height of the block with a metric ruler. Record your answers in cm.

Length (cm)	
Width (cm)	
Height (cm)	

3. Find the volume of the block, using the formula below:

   length × width × height = volume

   _____ **cm** × _____ **cm** × _____ **cm** = _____ **cm³**

4. What do you think will happen to the shape and volume of the block when it is placed in a container?

   _____

   _____

5. Place the block in the jar. What happened to the shape and volume of the block?

   _____

Conclusions

6. What state of matter is the wooden block in?

   _____

7. What are some other examples of objects in this state?

   _____

   _____

Investigation 2

What Is a Liquid?

Materials

- student record sheet on page 13, reproduced for each student

- water

- 250-mL beakers

- 100-mL graduated cylinders

Steps to Follow

1. Divide the class into small groups.

2. Give each group a 250-mL beaker filled with 100 mL of water. Have students note the shape and volume of the water in the beaker. Tell students that the volume of the water is measured in units called milliliters (mL). Have students record their data on their record sheets.

3. Ask students to recall what happens to the shape and volume of a solid when it is put into a container. Then have them predict what will happen to the shape and volume of the water when it is poured into another container. Have them record their predictions on their record sheets.

4. Tell students to pour the water from the beaker into the graduated cylinder. Ask students to note the shape and volume of the water in the cylinder.

5. Tell students that water is a liquid. A **liquid** is a substance that changes shape to fit the container it is in, but it does not change volume when moved from one container to another. Liquid is one of the states of matter.

Follow-Up

All liquids can be poured (flow), but students have probably noticed that some pour more slowly than others. This is due to a property called viscosity. Explain that the more viscous the liquid, the more it resists flowing. Ask students to think of some of the liquids used in cooking (water, cream, oil, molasses, etc.) and to rank them in order from least viscous to most viscous. Then encourage them to conduct an experiment to see if their predictions were correct.

What Is a Liquid?

Procedure and Observations

1. Look at the water in the beaker. What shape is the water?

   _____

2. What is the volume of water in the beaker? Record your answer in mL.

   _____

3. What happens to the shape and volume of a solid when it is put into a container? (Recall what you observed in the last investigation.)

   _____

   _____

4. What do you think will happen to the shape and volume of the water when it is poured into another container?

   _____

   _____

5. Pour the water from the beaker into the graduated cylinder. What happened to the shape and volume of the water?

   _____

   _____

Conclusions

6. What state of matter is the water in?

   _____

7. What are some other examples of objects in this state?

   _____

   _____

Concept

2

Simple Chemistry

Investigation 3

What Is a Gas?

Materials

- student record sheet on page 15, reproduced for each student
- long balloon (kind used for balloon sculptures)
- lidded glass jars (16-oz. [480-mL] or larger)
- paper towels
- books of matches

Steps to Follow

1. Blow up the balloon and tie it off. Hold it up for students to see. Elicit from students that the balloon is filled with air. Ask students what shape the air is inside the balloon. Then ask them to predict what will happen to the shape of the air when the balloon is bent into a different shape.

2. Bend the balloon into the shape of a pretzel. Hold up your balloon sculpture and ask students what shape the air has taken.

3. Divide students into small groups. Give each group a glass jar with a lid, a paper towel, and some matches.

4. Lead students to understand that the seemingly "empty" jar is actually filled with air. (If they need proof, skip to the Follow-Up activity below.)

5. Instruct students to roll up the paper towel, fold it in half, and light one end with a match. Have them drop the lit paper towel into the jar and screw on the lid. After a few seconds, the flame will go out.

   Caution: Warn students to use extreme care when working with matches and flames.

6. Tell students to let the jar sit for about 2 minutes while it fills with smoke. Explain that smoke consists of tiny particles of material that have not burned completely and are suspended (floating) in air. Ask students to predict what will happen to the smoke inside the jar when they remove the lid.

7. Tell students to remove the lid from the jar and observe what happens to the smoke. Ask them to infer what happens to the air inside the jar.

8. Tell students that air is a mixture of gases. A **gas** is a substance that has no definite shape or volume. It changes shape and volume to fill whatever container it's in, whether a balloon, a jar, or the classroom! Gas is one of the states of matter.

Follow-Up

How do we know an "empty" jar is filled with air? Have students remove the paper towel and ashes from the jar, turn it upside down over a clear bowl or pitcher of water, and push the jar straight down in the water. Water doesn't enter the jar because the jar is already filled with air.

What Is a Gas?

Procedure and Observations

1. Look at the balloon your teacher has blown up. What shape is the air inside the balloon?

   _____

2. What do you think will happen to the shape of the air when the balloon is bent or twisted into another shape?

   _____

3. Look at the balloon sculpture your teacher has made. What shape has the air inside the balloon taken?

   _____

4. Roll up a paper towel and light one end with a match. Drop it in the jar and screw on the lid. The flame will go out in a few seconds.

5. Watch as the jar fills with smoke. What do you think will happen to the smoke when the lid is removed?

   _____

6. Remove the lid. What happens to the smoke inside the jar?

   _____

7. What do you think happened to the air inside the jar?

   _____

Conclusions

8. What state of matter is air in?

   _____

9. What are some other examples of objects in this state?

   _____

   _____

Investigation 4

Changing States

Materials

- student record sheet on page 17, reproduced for each student
- overhead transparency of *States of Matter* on page 9
- 400-mL beaker
- hot plate
- access to a freezer
- ice cubes
- oven mitts

Steps to Follow

1. Review with students the three states of matter. Tell students that water is a substance that can exist in all three states: as a solid (ice), a liquid (water), and a gas (water vapor). Ask students what they think causes water to change state.

2. Pass around a beaker filled with ice cubes before placing it on a preheated hot plate. Ask students to observe the ice for several minutes and record what happens. (The ice will melt, forming water.)

3. Have students continue heating the water until it boils. Point out the bubbles in the water. Explain that these bubbles are steam—an invisible gas produced by vaporizing water (turning water to a vapor, or gas). Add that the fine mist or "cloud" above the boiling water is not steam, but tiny water droplets suspended in the air. These droplets form when the steam condenses—turns from a gas to a liquid. The "cloud" disappears as the droplets move farther and farther apart. Have students record their observations on their record sheets.

4. Tell students to continue boiling the water in the beaker until it is half gone. Ask students where the water went. Have them record their ideas on their record sheets.

5. Have students turn off the hot plate. After the water has cooled for several minutes, instruct a student volunteer to use oven mitts to place the beaker of water in a freezer. Ask students to predict what will happen to the water. They should record their predictions on their record sheets.

6. After several hours, have students check the state of the water in the freezer and record their observations.

7. Review students' results. Ask how they got the ice to melt, the water to boil and evaporate, and the rest of the water to freeze. Lead students to conclude that a substance can be changed from one state to another by heating or cooling it.

8. Using the *States of Matter* transparency, review with students what they have learned.

Changing States

Procedure and Observations

1. What are the three states of matter?

   _____

2. Water can exist in all three states. What do you think causes water to change state?

   _____

   _____

3. Place the beaker of ice cubes on a hot plate and turn it on. What happens to the ice after several minutes?

   _____

   _____

4. Bring the water in the beaker to a boil. Continue boiling the water until it is half gone. Where does the water go?

   _____

   _____

5. Turn off the hot plate. Once the water has cooled a bit, use oven mitts to place the beaker in the freezer.

6. After several hours, check on the water in the freezer. What has happened to it?

   _____

   _____

Conclusion

7. How did you get water to change state in this experiment?

   _____

   _____

   _____

Substances have characteristic properties.

Prepare in Advance

Investigation 1: Collect pan balances from around the school. (See image of pan balance on page 22.) Students will need them to find the mass of different objects and substances.

Investigation 2: Prepare two sets of objects for the class as follows:
Set I—wood, metal, and plastic objects, such as the following (all metal objects should be magnetic): plastic button, chalk, eraser, crayon, paper, blocks (wood, foam), marble, paper clip, thumbtack, scissors, bottle cap

Set II—metal objects, both magnetic and nonmagnetic: **magnetic**—safety pin, staples, tin can, stainless steel spoon; **nonmagnetic**—coins, aluminum foil, house keys, silver or gold jewelry

Investigation 3: Prepare samples of flour, sugar, baking soda, salt, and cornstarch in small cups, as directed on page 29.

Investigation 4: Collect chocolate, butter, and wax samples. Collect or prepare crushed ice. Make sure you have enough thermometers to carry out the investigation.

Investigation 5: Collect the equipment needed to construct the boiling point apparatuses (see page 34). Put one together yourself to use as a demonstration for the class. If you do not have a burette clamp and rubber stopper, you can use a rubber band to secure the thermometer to a wooden block and place the block in the beaker of water.

Teacher Information

A **characteristic property** is a physical or chemical property that is unique to a particular substance and can therefore be used to identify the substance and to distinguish it from other substances.

Density is the amount of matter in a given volume of substance—in other words, how compact a substance is. The denser the substance, the more matter packed into a given volume of the substance, and therefore the more it weighs. For example, wood is denser than foam. As a result, a wooden block will weigh more than a foam block of the same size. An equal-size lead block will weigh more than either the wooden or the foam block because lead is denser than wood and foam. To find the density of a substance, simply divide its mass by its volume: $D = m/V$.

Magnetism is the force of attraction between a magnet and a magnetic object. A **magnet** is an object that attracts iron or objects containing iron. An object is **magnetic** if it is attracted to a magnet or if it has the properties of a magnet. All magnets are surrounded by a magnetic field, which is an invisible force that can push or pull on magnetic objects from a distance. The magnetic field surrounding a magnet is produced by moving charged particles (electrons) within the atoms that make up the magnet. (For more information on atoms, see Concept 5.)

Solubility is a measure of the amount of a substance that can be dissolved in another substance, usually a solid dissolved in water. The **solute** is the substance that is dissolved. The **solvent** is the substance in which the solute dissolves. The resulting substance is called a **solution.** Some substances have a higher solubility than others. The higher the solubility, the more of the substance that can be dissolved in a given amount of solvent. In general, crystals are more soluble in liquids than powders.

The **melting point** of a substance is the temperature at which the substance changes from a solid to a liquid. The melting point of a substance is the same as its freezing point (the temperature at which the substance changes from a liquid to a solid). Some substances have melting points around room temperature; others melt at much lower temperatures.

The **boiling point** of a substance is the temperature at which the substance changes from a liquid to a gas by heating it. The boiling point of a substance is the same as its condensation point (the temperature at which the substance changes from a gas to a liquid).

Although melting and boiling are brought about by the application of heat, the temperature of a substance does not change while it is undergoing a change of state. For example, while a substance is melting, its temperature remains constant until it has finished melting. Then it increases again until it reaches its boiling point. Once a substance reaches its boiling point, its temperature will increase no further. Instead, it turns to a vapor.

The melting point and boiling point of a pure substance are constant unless impurities are added. For example, frozen water always melts at 0°C. Dissolving salt in water, however, changes the chemical composition of the water. The salt in effect lowers the melting point of the water. That's why salt is sprinkled on icy roads in winter—it lowers the temperature at which water turns to ice. So even when it's slightly below freezing, the roads will be wet, not icy. Salt also raises the boiling point of water.

Characteristic Properties

Physical and chemical properties that are unique to a particular substance.

Density:

The amount of matter in a given volume of substance. The denser the substance, the more it weighs per unit volume.

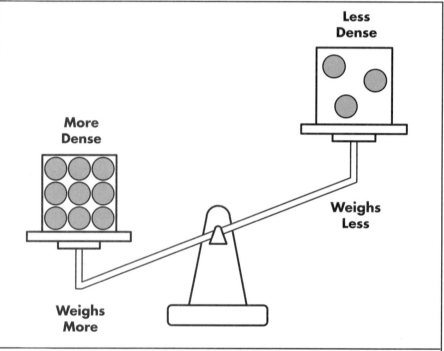

Less Dense

More Dense

Weighs Less

Weighs More

Magnetism:

The force of attraction between a magnet and a magnetic object.

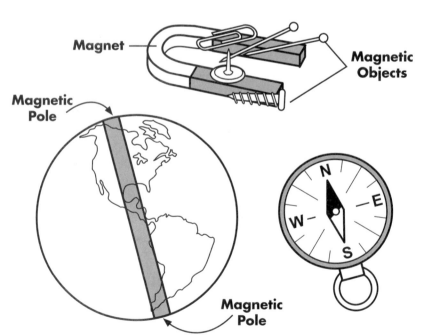

Magnet

Magnetic Objects

Magnetic Pole

Magnetic Pole

Solubility:

A measure of the amount of a substance that can be dissolved in another substance, usually a solid in water.

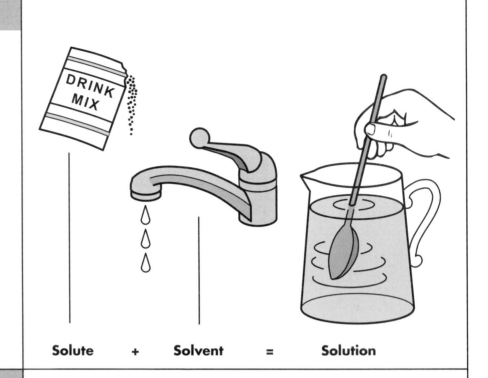

Solute   +   Solvent   =   Solution

Melting Point:

The temperature at which a substance changes from a solid to a liquid.

Boiling Point:

The temperature at which a substance changes from a liquid to a gas.

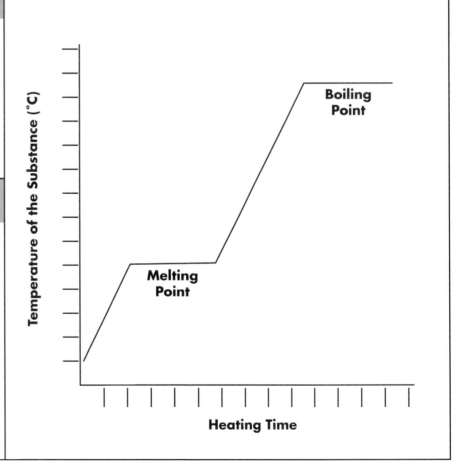

Simple Chemistry • EMC 878

Investigation 1

Density

Materials

See advance preparation on page 18.

- student record sheets on pages 24 and 25, reproduced for each student
- wooden blocks
- foam blocks
- 100-mL graduated cylinders
- vegetable oil
- water
- paper cups
- metric rulers
- balances

Steps to Follow

1. Tell students that **density** is the amount of matter in a given volume of substance. Different substances have different densities. You can find out how dense something is by dividing its mass by its volume ($D = m/V$).

2. Divide the class into small groups. Give each group a wooden block and a foam block.

3. Have them find the mass of each block by weighing it on a balance. Tell them that **mass** is the amount of matter in an object or substance. Mass is measured in units called **grams.**

4. Have students find the volume of each block by measuring and then multiplying length × width × height. The volume of the blocks is measured in cubic centimeters (cm^3).

5. Tell students to use the formula $D = m/V$ to find the density of the two blocks, which is measured in g/cm^3. Which is denser: the wooden block or the foam block? Have students record their observations on their record sheets.

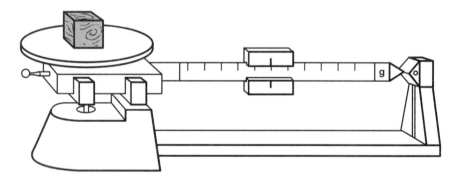

6. Now give students a graduated cylinder, 50 mL of water in one paper cup, and 50 mL of vegetable oil in another cup.

7. Have students place the empty graduated cylinder on the balance and reset the balance to zero. This is done so that their measurements are of the liquid only and do not include the mass of the cylinder.

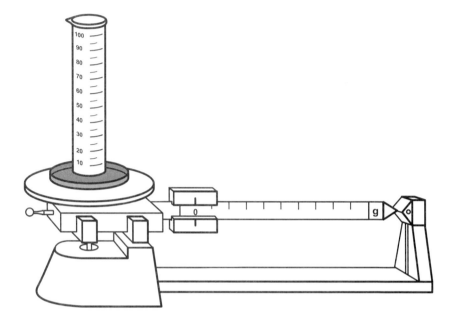

8. Tell students to find the mass of each liquid by pouring it into the cylinder and weighing.

9. Tell students to find the volume of each liquid by noting the level of the liquid in the cylinder. The volume of a liquid is measured in milliliters (mL).

10. Now have students use the formula $D = m/V$ to find the density of the two liquids, which is measured in g/mL. Which is denser: the water or the oil? Have students record their observations on their record sheets.

Follow-Up

Have students find the density of two "irregular" solids—a metal bolt and a rubber eraser—using the water displacement method. (An irregular solid is a solid whose sides are uneven or asymmetrical and whose dimensions therefore can't easily be measured.) Tell them to first find the mass of each object by weighing it on a balance. Tell them to then find the volume of each object by immersing it in a graduated cylinder filled with water and measuring the amount of water displaced by the object. (The volume of water displaced by an object is equal to the volume of the object.) Density found by the water displacement method is measured in g/mL. Which is denser: the bolt or the eraser?

Density

Procedure and Observations

1. Density is the amount of matter in a given volume of substance. Density = mass ÷ volume, or D = m/V.

2. This first exercise shows you how to find the density of a solid. To begin, find the mass of each block by weighing it on the balance.

   Mass of wooden block = _____ g

   Mass of foam block = _____ g

3. Find the volume of each block by measuring and then multiplying length × width × height.

   Dimensions of wooden block: length = _____ cm   width = _____ cm   height = _____ cm

   Dimensions of foam block: length = _____ cm   width = _____ cm   height = _____ cm

   Volume of wooden block = _____ cm^3

   Volume of foam block = _____ cm^3

4. Find the density of each block using the equation D = m/V.

   Density of wooden block = _____ g/cm^3

   Density of foam block = _____ g/cm^3

Conclusion

5. Which is denser: the wooden block or the foam block?

   _____

Procedure and Observations

6. This second exercise shows you how to find the density of a liquid. To begin, place the graduated cylinder on the balance and reset the balance to zero. Why do you think this is important?

_____

_____

7. Find the mass of each liquid by pouring it into the cylinder and weighing it on the balance.

   Mass of water = _____ g

   Mass of oil = _____ g

8. Find the volume of each liquid by noting the level of the liquid in the cylinder.

   Volume of water = _____ mL

   Volume of oil = _____ mL

9. Find the density of each liquid using the equation D = m/V.

   Density of water = _____ g/mL

   Density of oil = _____ g/mL

Conclusion

10. Which is denser: water or oil?

_____

Concept 3 · Simple Chemistry

Investigation 2

Magnetism

Materials

See advance preparation on page 18.

- student record sheets on pages 27 and 28, reproduced for each student
- magnets
- table or desk
- 2 sets of assorted objects to test

Steps to Follow

1. Tell students that **magnetism** is the force of attraction between a magnet and a magnetic object or substance. Ask students to describe any experiences they have had with magnets and magnetism.

2. Place the objects in Set I on a table or desk. Give students an opportunity to examine them. Ask students to predict which objects are magnetic and which are not. Have them record their predictions on the Set I chart on their record sheets.

3. Divide students into small groups. Give each group a magnet and tell them to test the objects on the table to determine which are magnetic. Have them hold the magnet close to each object and note whether they feel a "pulling force" between the object and the magnet. That pulling force means the object is magnetic.

4. Clear the table. Place the objects in Set II on the table. Ask students to predict which objects in this set are magnetic. They should record their predictions on the Set II chart on their record sheets.

5. Have students test the objects in Set II to determine which are magnetic.

6. Tell students that a **magnet** is an object that attracts iron (a metal) or objects/substances that contain iron. Ask students which of the objects in Sets I and II contain iron.

Follow-Up

Magnetic objects (objects that contain iron) can be magnetized to become temporary magnets themselves. Invite students to choose a magnetic object from either set. Tell them to rub a permanent magnet several times in the same direction along the length of the object. Doing so causes clusters of atoms, called domains, in the object to align and act like tiny magnets. Then have students use the magnetized object to test the magnetic properties of other objects.

Name _____

Magnetism

Procedure and Observations

1. Look at the first set of objects on the table. List each object on the chart below and predict whether it is magnetic. Then use a magnet to test the magnetic properties of each object and record your results on the chart.

Set I		
Object	Prediction: Do you think it's magnetic?	Result: Is it magnetic?

Conclusion

2. Other than their attraction to the magnet, what do all the magnetic objects in Set I have in common?

_____

_____

Procedure and Observations

3. Look at the second set of objects on the table. List each object in the chart below and predict whether it is magnetic. Then use the magnet to test the magnetic properties of each object and record your results on the chart.

Set II		
Object	**Prediction:** **Do you think it's magnetic?**	**Result:** **Is it magnetic?**

Conclusions

4. A magnet is an object that attracts iron. Which of the objects in Sets I and II contain iron?

_____

_____

5. Are all metal objects magnetic? Support your answer with evidence from the investigation.

_____

_____

Investigation 3

Solubility

Materials

See advance preparation on page 18.

- student record sheet on page 30, reproduced for each student
- tsp. measuring spoon
- all-purpose bleached flour
- table sugar (granulated)
- table salt (granulated)
- baking soda
- cornstarch
- stirring rods
- water
- 250-mL beakers
- small cups
- magnifiers
- masking tape
- markers

Steps to Follow

1. Ask students what happens when they stir drink mix into water. Explain that when a substance dissolves in water, its particles are broken down into their smallest possible size and float evenly between the water particles that surround them. The result is a **solution.**

2. Some solids dissolve better than others. **Solubility** is a measure of the amount of a substance that can be dissolved in another substance, usually water. Substances with a high solubility will seem to disappear into the water, while substances with a low solubility will turn the water cloudy, settle to the bottom, or float on top.

3. Divide the class into small groups. Give each group a magnifier and a teaspoon each of flour, sugar, baking soda, salt, and cornstarch in small, separate cups. Ask students to examine and rub a pinch of each between their fingers. Help them distinguish between a powder and a crystal. Ask them to predict what will happen to each substance when mixed with water. Tell them to record their predictions on the chart on their record sheet.

4. Have students fill five beakers with 100 mL of water each. Tell them to label the beakers with the name of each substance (flour, sugar, baking soda, salt, or cornstarch).

5. Instruct students to pour the contents of each cup into the corresponding beaker of water. Tell them to stir each sample for 2 minutes. Then allow the beakers and their contents to stand undisturbed for 2 more minutes.

6. Finally, have students record their observations on the chart. Which substances have a high solubility? Which have a low solubility?

Follow-Up

Have students investigate the relationship between solubility and temperature. Have them compare how much salt or sugar they can dissolve in equal amounts of hot water and cold water. (Students should find that, for these substances, hot water dissolves more solute.)

Name _____

Solubility

Procedure and Observations

1. Examine the flour, sugar, baking soda, salt, and cornstarch with a magnifier. Rub a pinch of each between your fingers. Is it a powder or a crystal? What do you think will happen to each substance when it is mixed with water? Record your predictions on the chart below.

2. Fill five beakers with 100 mL of water each. Label the beakers. Pour the contents of each cup into the corresponding beaker and stir for 2 minutes. Then let each beaker stand for 2 minutes.

3. Observe the contents of each beaker and record your observations on the chart.

Substance	Powder or crystal?	Prediction: What will happen when mixed with water?	Observation: What happened when mixed with water?	High solubility or low solubility?
flour				
sugar				
baking soda				
salt				
cornstarch				

Conclusion

4. Based on your results, which seems to dissolve more easily: powders or crystals?

_____

Investigation 4

Melting Point

Materials

See advance preparation on page 18.

• student record sheet on page 32, reproduced for each student

• 400-mL beaker

• test tubes

• thermometers

• crushed ice

• butter

• chocolate

• wax

• hot plate

• cold water

Steps to Follow

1. Tell students that the temperature at which a substance melts (changes from a solid to a liquid) is its **melting point.** Ask students if they think all solids melt at the same temperature.

2. Have students fill a beaker with 250 mL of cold water and set it on a hot plate.

3. Next, give students equal-size chunks of chocolate, butter, wax, and crushed ice. Tell students to place each substance in a different test tube and place the test tubes in the beaker of water.

4. Have students insert a thermometer into the center of each sample. (If the sample is hard, students can wait for it to soften or begin melting.) Tell them they are going to heat the tubes. Ask students to predict which substance will melt first and which will melt last. Have them record their predictions on their record sheets.

5. Tell students to turn on the hot plate to medium heat and observe the contents of each tube. The temperature of each substance will rise, then level off as the substance melts, then begin rising again on its way to boiling. Tell them to record this "plateau" temperature in the table. This is the true melting point of the substance.

6. When students have finished, have them rank the substances from lowest to highest melting point.

Follow-Up

Students know what the melting point of ice is. Ask them if they know what the freezing point of water is. (Freezing point is the temperature at which a liquid turns to a solid.) Have students place a thermometer in a beaker of water, then place the beaker in the freezer. Tell them to note the temperature at which the water begins to freeze. What can they conclude about the melting point and freezing point of a substance? (They are the same.)

Melting Point

Procedure and Observations

1. The temperature at which a substance changes from a solid to a liquid is its melting point. Do you think all solids melt at the same temperature? How do you know?

   _____

   _____

2. Fill a beaker with 250 mL of cold water. Place the beaker on a hot plate.

3. Place the chocolate, butter, wax, and crushed ice in separate test tubes. Place the test tubes in the beaker of water.

4. Insert a thermometer in each test tube. Which substance do you think will begin to melt first? Which do you think will begin to melt last?

   _____

   _____

5. Turn on the hot plate to medium heat. Take the temperature of each substance as it is melting. Record the melting point of each substance.

Substance	Melting Point (°C)
chocolate	
butter	
wax	
crushed ice	

Conclusions

6. Which substance has the lowest melting point? Which has the highest melting point?

   _____

7. Which substances are solid at room temperature (22°C)? Which are liquid?

   _____

Concept
3
Simple Chemistry

Investigation 5

Boiling Point

Materials

See advance preparation on page 18.

- student record sheets on pages 35–37, reproduced for each student
- goggles
- 400-mL beakers
- rubber stoppers
- burette clamps and stands
- table salt
- Tbsp. measuring spoon
- hot plate
- water

Steps to Follow

1. Tell students that the temperature at which a substance boils (changes from a liquid to a gas by being heated) is its **boiling point.** Ask students if they know what the boiling point of water is.

2. Tell students to pour 250 mL of water in a beaker and place the beaker on a hot plate.

3. Have students insert a thermometer into a rubber stopper, and the stopper in a burette clamp. The clamp should then be attached to the clamp stand. (See image of completed apparatus on page 34.)

4. Tell students to position the thermometer inside the beaker of water so that the bulb is about 2 centimeters above the bottom of the beaker. (It is important to keep the bulb of the thermometer from touching the bottom or sides of the beaker.)

5. Have students put on their safety goggles. Tell students to turn on the hot plate to medium heat and record the temperature of the water every half-minute (30 seconds) until well after the water has begun to boil. They should note that the temperature of the water rises, then levels off. This "plateau" temperature is the boiling point of water.

6. Help students as needed to graph the temperature change on their record sheets. Remind them that 30 seconds is equivalent to 0.5 minutes.

7. Next, ask students if they think the boiling point of a substance can ever change.

8. Have students add two tablespoons of salt to the water, let the water continue boiling for several minutes, then record the temperature of the water on the chart.

9. Have students repeat this step two more times and record the temperature each time.

10. When students have finished, ask them what effect adding salt has on the boiling point of water. (It raises the boiling point.)

Follow-Up

Have students repeat the experiment with sugar instead of salt. They should discover that it is the amount of particles dissolved in a substance—not the nature of the particles—that changes the boiling point of the substance.

Boiling Point Apparatus

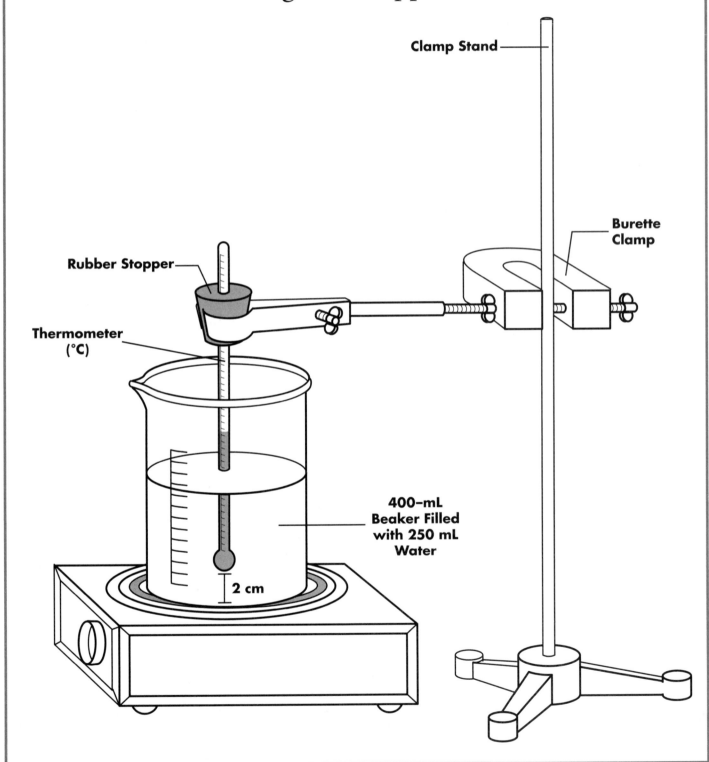

Clamp Stand

Burette Clamp

Rubber Stopper

Thermometer (°C)

400–mL Beaker Filled with 250 mL Water

2 cm

Name ______________________________

Concept 3 Simple Chemistry

Investigation 5

Boiling Point

Procedure and Observations

1. The temperature at which a substance changes from a liquid to a gas is its boiling point. What do you think the boiling point of water is?

   ____

2. Pour 250 mL of water in a beaker. Place the beaker on a hot plate.

3. Insert the thermometer into a rubber stopper. Attach the stopper to a burette clamp. Then attach the clamp to the clamp stand.

4. Turn on the hot plate to medium heat. Measure the temperature of the water every half-minute (30 seconds) until well after the water has begun to boil. Record the temperatures on the chart at right.

Time (min.)	Temperature (°C)
0.0	
0.5	
1.0	
1.5	
2.0	
2.5	
3.0	
3.5	
4.0	
4.5	
5.0	
5.5	
6.0	
6.5	
7.0	
7.5	
8.0	
8.5	
9.0	
9.5	
10.0	

5. Graph your data using the grid below.

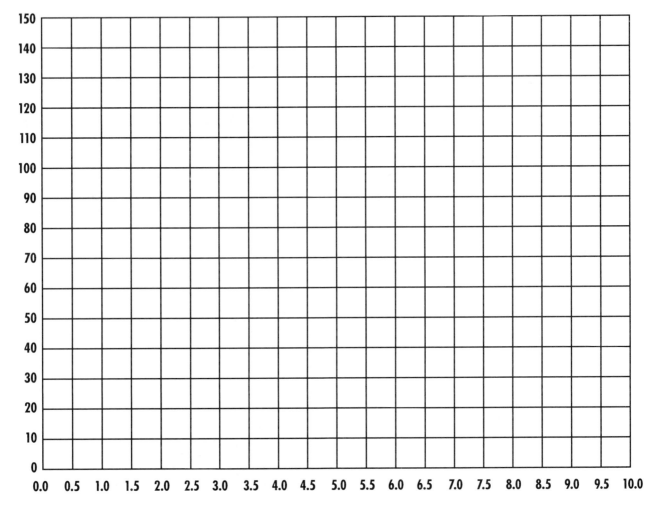

6. Now add 24 g of salt to the water. Let the water boil for several minutes, then record the temperature of the water.

7. Repeat this step two more times.

Substance	Boiling Point (°C)
250 mL water	
250 mL water + 24 g salt	
250 mL water + 48 g salt	
250 mL water + 72 g salt	

Conclusions

8. What is the boiling point of water?

_____

9. What effect does adding salt have on the boiling point of water?

_____

_____

_____

Mixtures can sometimes be separated into the original substances using characteristic properties.

Prepare in Advance

Investigation 1: Assemble lab kits containing the following materials for each group: goggles, beaker, stirring rod, magnet, filter paper, funnel, magnifier, and some water.

Teacher Information

Most of the objects and substances around you are not pure but rather mixtures or compounds. A **mixture** is a combination of different substances whose physical and chemical properties do not change despite being mixed together. The components of a mixture retain their identity and may be present in any proportion. Sand is an example of a mixture made of loose, grain-size pieces of rocks, minerals, and shells.

A **compound** is formed when two or more substances combine chemically to produce an entirely new substance. The properties of a compound are different from the properties of the substances from which it is made. Consider the compound formed when a sodium (Na) atom and a chlorine (Cl) atom chemically combine. Sodium is a soft, malleable metal that reacts explosively with water. Chlorine is a poisonous greenish-yellow gas. Together they form sodium chloride (NaCl)—ordinary table salt.

Unlike the components in a mixture, the components in a compound are always in a fixed proportion. Changing the ratio of the components changes the compound to something else. For example, carbon dioxide (CO_2), made by combining one carbon atom with two oxygen atoms, is a byproduct of respiration. Carbon monoxide (CO), which consists of one atom each of carbon and oxygen, is a deadly gas.

The components of a compound cannot be separated except by chemical means. The components of a mixture, however, can be separated by exploiting one or more of the physical properties that distinguish each component, such as size, density, solubility, magnetic properties, high or low boiling point, and so on. Some of the methods of separating the components of a mixture include sifting with a sieve, filtration, dialysis, dissolving and then washing away soluble solids, precipitation (converting dissolved substances back to solids), distillation, evaporation, condensation, floatation (used with substances of different densities), and chromatography (selective absorption). In this section, students get to use some of these techniques to isolate the components of several mixtures.

Mixture v. Compound

Pure Substance

Made of only one kind of matter.

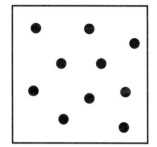 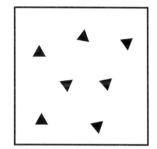

Mixture

Combination of two or more substances that keep their properties despite being mixed together.

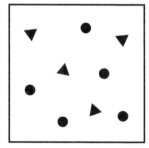

Compound

New substance formed when two or more substances chemically combine.

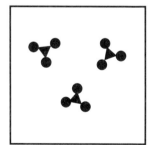

Concept 4 · Simple Chemistry

Investigation 1

All Mixed Up

Materials

See advance preparation on page 38.

• student record sheet on page 41, reproduced for each student

• goggles

• 400-mL beakers

• stirring rods

• iron filings

• paper clips

• table sugar

• sand

• water

• paper cups

• magnets

• filter paper

• funnels

• magnifiers

Steps to Follow

1. Divide students into small groups. Distribute a lab kit to each group.

2. Give each group samples of iron filings, table sugar, sand, and paper clips—each in a separate paper cup. Tell students to use the materials in their lab kits to examine each substance. Have them record the properties of each substance on the chart on their record sheets.

3. Instruct students to combine the four substances in a beaker and stir until thoroughly blended. Tell students that they have just made a mixture. A **mixture** is a combination of different substances whose characteristic properties do not change despite being mixed together. Explain that their next task is to figure out how to separate each substance from the mixture.

4. Have students outline the steps they will use to separate the components of their mixture and submit it for your approval. (Students might suggest that they can remove the paper clips by hand, separate out the filings using a magnet, and separate the sand from the sugar by dissolving the sugar in water and filtering out the sand.)

5. Instruct students to carry out their experiments. Tell them to record the most effective method for isolating each substance, and to identify the property of each substance that made it possible for them to do so.

Follow-Up

Encourage students to come up with their own mixture recipes, and then challenge another team to try to separate the components. Check mixture recipes before students assemble them. Remind students that each component must be able to be separated out using a simple procedure like filtering or dissolving.

Name _____

All Mixed Up

Procedure and Observations

1. Examine the iron filings, table sugar, sand, and paper clips. Record some properties of each substance on the chart below.

2. Pour all four substances into a dry beaker and mix thoroughly. Note that the properties of each substance in the beaker have not changed. That's what makes this a mixture. You are going to use some of these properties to help you separate out the substances in the mixture.

3. On the back of this sheet, list the steps you will use to separate the four substances in the mixture. Let your teacher review your plan.

4. Once your teacher has approved your plan, begin separating the substances. When you have finished, record the method you used to separate each substance, and the property of the substance that made separation possible.

Substance	Properties of substance	Method used to separate substance from mixture	Property that made separation possible
iron filings			
table sugar			
sand			
paper clips			

Investigation 2

Density Differences

Materials

- student record sheet on page 43, reproduced for each student
- 400-mL beakers
- wooden blocks
- bolts
- water
- vegetable oil
- sawdust or pencil shavings
- iron filings
- paper cups

Steps to Follow

1. Divide the class into small groups.

2. Tell each group to fill a beaker with water and place a wooden block and a metal bolt in the water. Ask students if the objects sink or float. Have them record their observations on their record sheets. (The wooden block will float while the bolt will sink.)

3. Explain that an object or substance that is less dense than water will float in it, while an object or substance that is denser than water will sink. Ask students which is denser: the block or the water, the bolt or the water, the block or the bolt.

4. Tell students to empty the beaker. Then have them pour equal amounts of water and oil in the beaker and let it sit for a minute. Ask students what happens to the oil and water, and which of the liquids is denser. (The oil will settle out in a layer above the water, as it is less dense than water.)

5. Point out that students can use differences in density to separate mixtures. Give students a mixture of sawdust and iron filings in a paper cup. Challenge them to separate the two components of the mixture using density differences. (If students place the mixture in a clean beaker of water, the filings will sink while the sawdust floats.) Ask students which is denser: the iron filings or the sawdust.

Follow-Up

Tell students to fill a beaker with half water and half oil, then drop the bolt and the block in the beaker. Ask students to rank the water, oil, bolt, and block in order from most dense to least dense (bolt, water, oil, wooden block).

Name _____

Density Differences

Procedure and Observations

1. Fill a beaker with water. Place the block and the bolt in the water. What happens to the block? What happens to the bolt?

_____

_____

_____

2. If an object or substance floats in water, it is less dense than the water. If an object or substance sinks, it is denser than water. Which of the following is denser? Circle the correct choice.

   The **block** or the **water**?   The **bolt** or the **water**?   The **block** or the **bolt**?

3. Empty the beaker. Then pour water and vegetable oil in the beaker. What happens to the water? What happens to the oil?

_____

_____

4. Which is denser: the water or the oil?

_____

5. Use density differences to separate a mixture of iron filings and sawdust. Describe your setup below.

_____

_____

6. How did you separate the filings from the sawdust?

_____

_____

7. Which is denser: the sawdust or the iron filings?

_____

Investigation 3

Paper Chromatography

Materials

- student record sheets on pages 46 and 47, reproduced for each student
- water soluble markers (black, blue, red, green)
- coffee filters
- scissors
- metric rulers
- 400-mL beakers
- water

Steps to Follow

1. Divide students into small groups. Give each group a black, a blue, a red, and a green water-soluble marker. Tell students that different colors of ink were mixed together to make the color in each marker. Ask students to predict which colors were mixed to make each marker. Have them record their ideas on their record sheets. Then tell students they are going to perform a simple scientific procedure to find out.

2. Have students cut four strips from the coffee filter, each about 15 cm long and about 2 cm wide. Tell students to draw a black dot about the diameter of a pencil approximately 2 cm from the end of one strip. Then have them draw a blue dot the same size and location on a second strip, a green dot on the third, and a red dot on the fourth.

3. Instruct students to place the filter strips in the beaker, dotted-end down, and fold the opposite end of each strip over the beaker rim to hold it in place. The dotted end of each strip should be about 1 cm from the bottom of the beaker.

4. Now have students pour a small amount of water into the beaker, enough so that the end of each strip just touches the water. Students should observe the strips absorb water. As the water passes through the colored dot, it will carry some of the color with it up the strip.

5. Tell students to wait about 15 minutes, then observe the strips again. They should discover that each colored dot has separated into different colors. Have students record these colors on the chart on their record sheets.

6. Explain that **chromatography** is the process of separating a mixture (a solution) by passing it through an absorbing material. The different components of the mixture are absorbed at different rates, which causes them to separate. The rate at which each component flows through the absorbing material is called the **flow rate.** The color at the top of each strip has the fastest flow rate. The color at the bottom has the slowest flow rate.

7. Have students examine each strip. Which of the colors in the black marker has the fastest flow rate? The slowest? For the blue marker? Green marker? Red marker? Tell students to record their answers on the chart.

Follow-Up

Have students use chromatography to determine the pigments contained in green leaves. Have students crush a green leaf and rub it on the end of a filter strip. Then have them dip the end of the strip in isopropyl alcohol or acetone (nail polish remover). Students may be surprised to see the green stain separate into one or more of the following: yellow, orange, brown, red, and purple, depending on the type of leaf used.

Paper Chromatography

Procedure and Observations

1. The black, blue, red, and green ink in the markers was made by mixing together different colors of ink. What colors do you think were used to make the

   black ink? _____

   blue ink? _____

   red ink? _____

   green ink? _____

2. Cut four strips from the coffee filter. Draw a black dot on one, a blue dot on another, a red dot on the third, and a green dot on the fourth.

3. Place the strips dotted-end down in the beaker and fold the opposite end over the rim.

4. Pour a small amount of water into the beaker—just enough to wet the ends of the strips below the dots. Don't pour too much! What happens to the strips?

   _____

   _____

5. What happens to the colored dot on each strip as the water begins to touch it?

   _____

   _____

6. Let your beaker sit for about 15 minutes.

7. After 15 minutes, look at the strips again. What colors has each dot separated into? Record your observations on the chart.

Dot color	Separates into these colors (Write in order from top to bottom of strip.)	Color with fastest flow rate	Color with slowest flow rate
black			
blue			
red			
green			

Conclusion

8. Chromatography is a method of separating the components of a solution by passing it through an absorbing material. Each component flows at a different rate, with the fastest-flowing component ending up at the top of the strip and the slowest at the bottom. Which color in each marker has the fastest flow rate? Which has the slowest? Record your answers on the chart.

 Simple Chemistry • EMC 878

Elements are organized in the periodic table.

Prepare in Advance

Investigation 2: Make arrangements to have a chart of the periodic table on a classroom wall.

Investigation 3: You will need to copy the game board found on pages 66 and 67 for each group. The empty boxes on the board correspond to the size of the game tiles found on pages 63–65.

Teacher Information

Every object and substance in the universe is made of matter. Recall that matter is anything that has mass and takes up space. But what is matter made of? And what makes one kind of matter different from another?

The smallest unit of matter is called an **atom.** In the **nucleus,** or center region, of every atom are one or more protons and neutrons*. A **proton** is a positively charged particle. A **neutron** is a particle that has no electric charge; in other words, it is neutral.

Located outside the nucleus are one or more negatively charged particles called **electrons.** Electrons travel around the nucleus at fixed distances, called **energy levels,** or **shells.** An atom can have up to seven energy levels, with each level capable of holding a different number of electrons.

The attraction between the positively charged protons and the negatively charged electrons is what holds the atom together. But because the number of protons in an atom always equals the number of electrons, the charges cancel each other out, and the atom itself is neutral.

An atom is identified by the number of protons in its nucleus. The number of protons in the nucleus of an atom determines its **atomic number.** For example, carbon has six protons in its nucleus. The atomic number for carbon is six.

Carbon is an example of an element. An **element** is a substance that cannot be broken down without changing the identity of the substance. For example, if you could somehow remove three protons from the nucleus of a carbon atom, you would end up with an atom whose nucleus contained three protons. An atom with an atomic number of three is called lithium.

Atoms combine in different ways to form different kinds of matter. Some kinds of matter are made up of only one kind of atom (one element). Other kinds of matter are made of two or more kinds of atoms (two or more elements) that have chemically combined. A substance made of two or more elements is called a **compound.** Elements and compounds make up all the different kinds of matter in the universe.

A hydrogen atom contains one proton, no neutrons, and one electron. It is the only element with no neutrons in the nucleus of its atoms.

Russian chemist Dmitri Ivanovich Mendeleyev was the first to arrange the elements by their properties. In 1869 he developed the **periodic table of the elements.** This chart consists of boxes, each of which contains information about a different element: the name and symbol, atomic number, and atomic mass. Some tables also contain information about the number of electrons in each energy level of an element's atoms.

The elements are arranged by increasing atomic number in horizontal rows called **periods.** But there's more to the story than that. As the atomic number increases, so must the number of electrons increase so that the element continues to be electrically neutral.

The chemical properties of an element are determined by the number and arrangement of its electrons, specifically those in the outermost shell of its atoms. Mendeleyev observed that although some elements had different atomic numbers, they shared many physical and chemical characteristics. As a result of this repetition or periodicity of characteristics, he grouped these elements into **families.** In the periodic table, families are represented by vertical columns.

In these investigations, students will learn the parts of an atom and make models of different kinds of atoms. Then they'll examine the periodic table and play a game that tests their knowledge of how the periodic table is arranged.

Model of a Carbon Atom

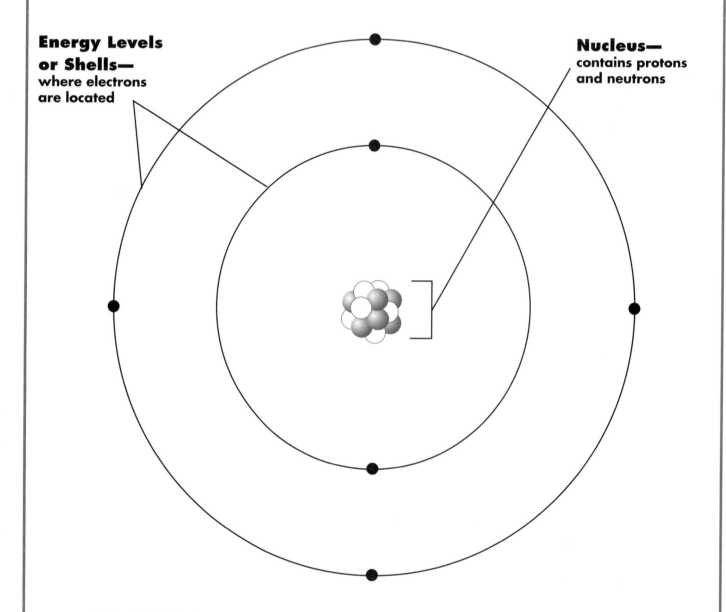

Energy Levels or Shells— where electrons are located

Nucleus— contains protons and neutrons

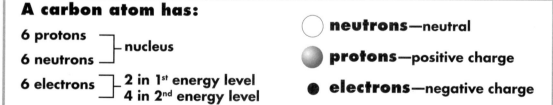

A carbon atom has:

6 protons ⎤
6 neutrons ⎦ nucleus

6 electrons ⎤ 2 in 1st energy level
⎦ 4 in 2nd energy level

◯ **neutrons**—neutral

🔘 **protons**—positive charge

● **electrons**—negative charge

A Very Brief History of Atomic Theory

c. 460 B.C.E.: Democritus (Greek philosopher)

Proposed that matter cannot be broken down indefinitely. At some point you end up with a piece that can't be divided. That smallest piece he called an atom, from the Greek word *atomos,* which means "indivisible."

1807: John Dalton (British chemist)

The first modern scientist to propose the existence of atoms. He described an atom as an invisible, indestructible, solid sphere, like a billiard ball.

1898: Sir Joseph John (J.J.) Thomson (British physicist)

Proposed the "plum-pudding" model: An atom is a solid mass of positively charged material with negative charges (electrons) scattered through it like pieces of plum in pudding. He is credited with discovering the electron.

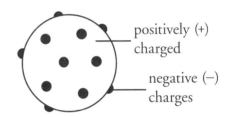

1911: Ernest Rutherford (British physicist)

His experiments proved that atoms are mostly empty space. Discovered the nucleus, which contains positively charged particles. Was the first to suggest that electrons circle the dense nucleus.

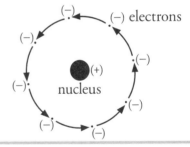

1913: Niels Bohr (Danish physicist)

Proposed that electrons move in different orbits, or energy levels, around the nucleus like planets orbit the sun. Each energy level is located a specific distance from the nucleus and contains a certain number of electrons.

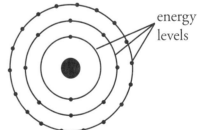

Current Atomic Model

Based on the Bohr model, except that electrons orbit the nucleus in random paths. The regions where they are most likely to be found are called electron clouds.

Periodic Table of the Elements

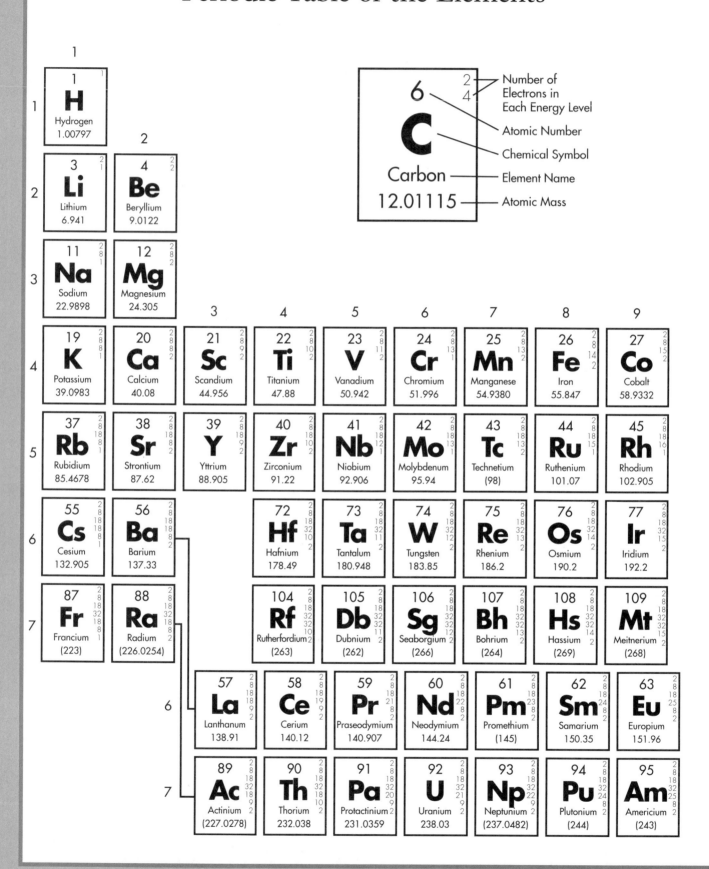

©2002 by Evan-Moor Corp.

Simple Chemistry • EMC 878

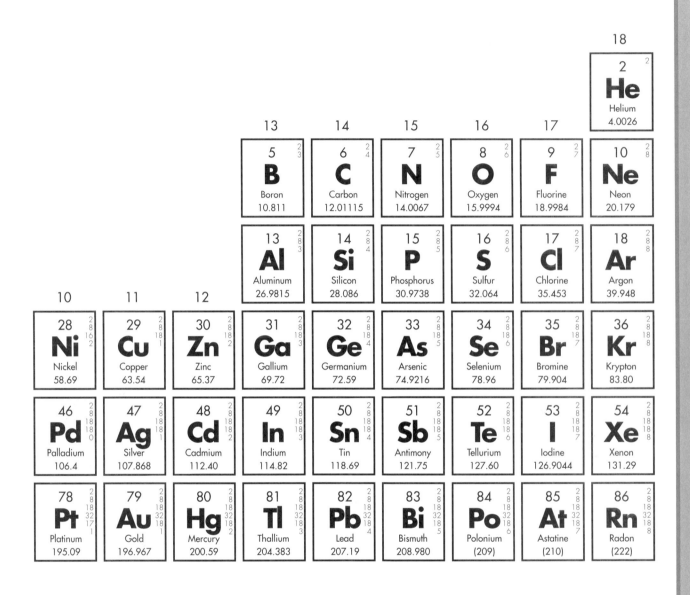

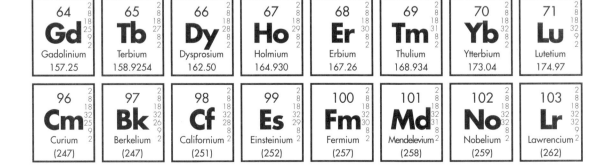

Concept 5 · Simple Chemistry

Investigation 1

Atomic Structure

Materials

- student record sheets on pages 56 and 57, reproduced for each student
- overhead transparency of *Model of a Carbon Atom* on page 50
- 2 glass mixing bowls, same size
- modeling clay, 3 different colors
- plastic wrap

Steps to Follow

1. When making copies of the *Atomic Template* on page 56, enlarge the image a bit so that students will have plenty of room for their clay balls.

2. Tell students that all matter is made up of atoms. An **atom** is the smallest unit of matter. Tell students that you are going to make a three-dimensional (3-D) model of an atom.

3. Explain that every atom has a **nucleus**—a center region—that contains one or more protons and neutrons. A **proton** is a positively charged particle in the nucleus of an atom. A **neutron** is a particle that has no charge (is neutral). To build a model nucleus, roll two clay balls, about the size of a thumbnail, to represent protons. Roll two more clay balls the same size but a different color to represent neutrons. Stick the four clay balls together. Set aside the model nucleus for now.

4. Using a third color of clay, roll two tiny balls to represent electrons. Tell students that **electrons** are negatively charged particles located outside the nucleus of an atom. Gently press one electron to the inside of each glass bowl. Cover one bowl with plastic wrap. Place the model nucleus in the center of the plastic wrap. Place the second bowl upside down on the first bowl. This forms a 3-D model of a helium atom.

5. Tell students that helium is an element. An **element** is a pure substance, which means it is made of only one kind of atom. There are approximately 110 known elements in the universe. Different elements are made of different atoms. Different atoms have different numbers of protons, neutrons, and electrons.

6. Make a model of a carbon atom by adding four protons and four neutrons to the nucleus of the model, for a total of six protons and six neutrons. Then place four more electrons on the outside of the glass bowls, for a total of six electrons (two on the inside and four on the outside).

7. Tell students that the electrons in an atom are arranged in different **energy levels,** or **shells.** Each level can hold only a certain number of electrons. In the case of the carbon atom, two electrons are in the first energy level and four are in the second. Some atoms have up to seven energy levels.

8. Show students the overhead transparency of the carbon atom model. Use it to review what students have just learned about atomic structure.

9. Give students three different colors of clay and tell them to use their atomic templates to model the atomic structure of the elements listed on part 2 of their record sheets. Tell students to make the protons and neutrons pea-size, and the electrons somewhat smaller.

Follow-Up

Have students work in groups to make atomic models of the following elements (draw a large template on the board and have students stick clay balls to the board):

Element	Number of Protons	Number of Neutrons	Number of Electrons at Each Energy Level
Titanium	22	22	2, 8, 10, 2
Iodine	53	53	2, 8, 18, 18, 7
Gold	79	79	2, 8, 18, 32, 18, 1
Uranium	92	92	2, 8, 18, 32, 21, 9, 2
Bohrium	107	107	2, 8, 18, 32, 32, 13, 2

Concept

5

Simple Chemistry

Investigation 1

Atomic Structure

Atomic Template

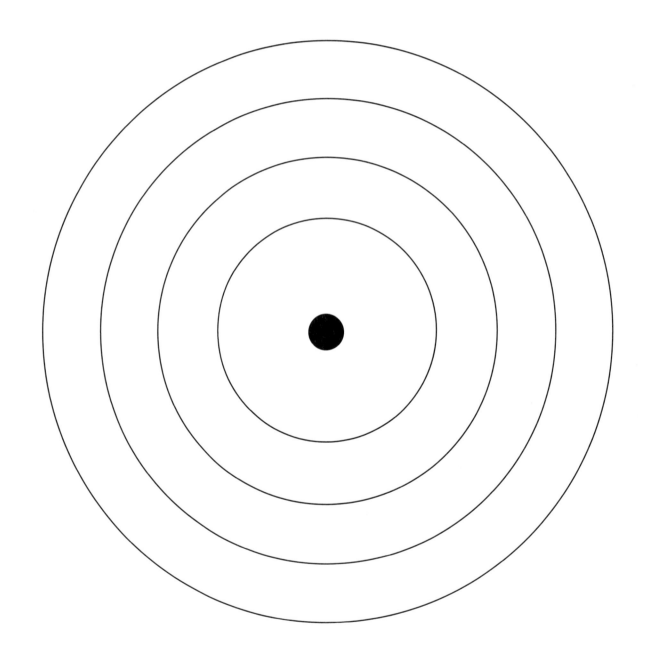

Procedure:

1. Use clay balls and the *Atomic Template* to create model atoms of the elements shown on the chart below.

Element	Number of Protons	Number of Neutrons	Number of Electrons in Each Energy Level
Hydrogen	1	0	1
Helium	2	2	2
Lithium	3	3	2, 1
Beryllium	4	4	2, 2
Boron	5	5	2, 3
Carbon	6	6	2, 4
Nitrogen	7	7	2, 5
Oxygen	8	8	2, 6
Fluorine	9	9	2, 7
Neon	10	10	2, 8
Sodium	11	11	2, 8, 1
Magnesium	12	12	2, 8, 2
Aluminum	13	13	2, 8, 3
Silicon	14	14	2, 8, 4
Phosphorus	15	15	2, 8, 5
Sulfur	16	16	2, 8, 6
Chlorine	17	17	2, 8, 7
Argon	18	18	2, 8, 8
Potassium	19	19	2, 8, 8, 1
Calcium	20	20	2, 8, 8, 2

Investigation 2

Looking at the Periodic Table

Materials

See advance preparation on page 48.

- student record sheets on pages 60 and 61, reproduced for each student
- periodic table on pages 52 and 53, reproduced for each student
- periodic table chart

Steps to Follow

1. Tell students that in 1869, Russian chemist Dmitri Mendeleyev organized all the known elements into a chart according to their properties. This chart is called the **periodic table of the elements.**

2. Distribute copies of the periodic table to each student. Have students look at the table. Explain that the periodic table is made up of boxes, each of which contains information about a different element. That information includes the name of the element, the one- or two-letter **atomic symbol,** the **atomic number** (the number of protons in the nucleus of an atom of that element), and the **atomic mass** (mass of an atom of that element, measured in atomic mass units, or amu).

3. Tell students that some versions of the table—like this one—also include the number of electrons in each energy level. Have students examine one box. Ask what they notice about the atomic number and the total number of electrons in an atom of that element. (They are the same.)

4. As a class, have students take turns reading the name of each element, from left to right, starting at the top left corner of the table. Help them pronounce the names when necessary.

5. Point out that the elements in the periodic table are arranged in horizontal rows called **periods.** Ask students how many periods there are and how many elements are in each period. Have a student volunteer read, in order, the names of the elements in periods 4 and 5.

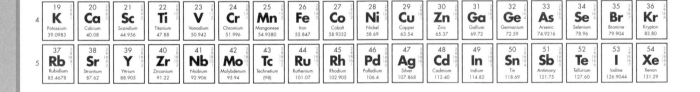

6. Next, ask students what they notice about the atomic numbers in each period. (The elements are arranged by increasing atomic number.) Ask what they notice, generally, about the atomic mass of the elements in each period. (With a few exceptions, it increases with an increase in the atomic number.) Ask students what they notice about the number of energy levels an element has and the period it's in. (The period number corresponds to the number of energy levels.)

7. Tell students that the elements are also arranged in vertical columns called **families** (or **groups**). Elements with similar physical and chemical properties are in the same family. Ask students how many families there are and how many elements are in each family. Have student volunteers read, in order, the names of the elements in families 1 and 2.

8. Have students answer the remaining questions about the periodic table on their record sheets.

Follow-Up

Challenge students to "discover" a new element and add it to the periodic table. What do they call their element? What is its symbol? What is the atomic number and mass, and how many electrons are in each energy level? Tell students to find an appropriate location for their element in the periodic table and to make sure it fits there.

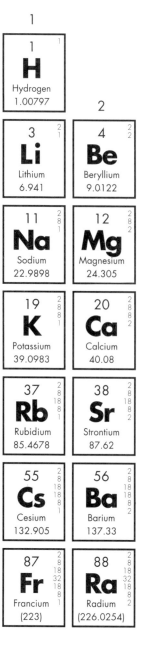

Name _____

Looking at the Periodic Table

Procedure and Observations

1. Look at the periodic table. Use it to answer the following questions.

2. What do you notice about the atomic number and the total number of electrons in an atom of that element?

   _____

   _____

3. How many periods are there?

   _____

4. What do you notice about the atomic number in each period?

   _____

   _____

5. In general, what happens to the atomic mass in each period?

   _____

   _____

6. What do you notice about the number of energy levels in an atom of an element and the period the element is in?

   _____

   _____

7. How many families are there?

   _____

8. How many elements are listed on the periodic table?

   _____

9. How many elements have an atomic number greater than that of iodine?

   _____

10. How many protons are in the nucleus of an atom of samarium?

    _____

11. Which element has more protons in the nucleus of its atoms: tin or lead?

    _____

12. What is the atomic symbol for:

    fluorine? _____ seaborgium? _____

13. Which element is represented by:

    U? _____ Ag? _____

14. Which element has the smallest atomic mass? The largest atomic mass?

    _____

15. What is the total number of electrons in an atom of osmium?

    _____

16. How many electrons are in the fifth energy level of a fermium atom?

    _____

17. To which period and family does promethium belong?

    _____

Investigation 3

Elements Game

Materials

See advance preparation on page 48.

- *Elements Game Tiles* on pages 63–65, reproduced for each group
- *Elements Game Board* on pages 66 and 67, reproduced for each group
- scissors

Steps to Follow

Note: In order to play this game, students must have completed Investigation 2: Looking at the Periodic Table.

1. Tell students that they are going to use what they have learned about how the periodic table of elements is organized to play a game.

2. Organize students into groups of four. Give each group sheets of the *Elements Game Tiles* and the *Elements Game Board*. Tell students to cut out the game tiles and shuffle them.

3. Challenge students to place all the tiles in the right location on the game board, using the clue printed on each tile. That clue might be the atomic number, atomic mass, number of electrons in each energy level, or the period and family of the element. The first group to fill in the table correctly wins.

4. You might want to offer this hint before students begin: Tell students that they may want to save the tiles with the atomic mass clues for last.

Follow-Up

Invite students to play a game of "Tic Tac Titanium." Working in pairs, have students shuffle a deck of game tiles and place them facedown. Players take turns drawing a tile and matching it to the corresponding box on the periodic table printed on pages 52 and 53. The first player to get all the elements in a period or a family wins.

Concept **5** Simple Chemistry

Elements Game
Tiles

1 **H** Hydrogen	**He** Helium 4.0026	**Li** ² ¹ Lithium	**Be** Beryllium Period:2 Family:13	**5** **B** Boron	**C** Carbon 12.01115	**N** ² ⁵ Nitrogen	**O** Oxygen Period:2 Family:16	**9** **F** Fluorine
Ne Neon 20.179	**Na** ² ⁸ ¹ Sodium	**Mg** Magnesium Period:3 Family:2	**13** **Al** Aluminum	**Si** Silicon 28.086	**P** ² ⁸ ⁵ Phosphorus	**S** Sulfur Period:3 Family:16	**17** **Cl** Chlorine	**Ar** Argon Period:3 Family:18
K ² ⁸ ⁸ ¹ Potassium	**21** **Ca** Calcium 40.08	**Sc** Scandium	**Ti** Titanium Period:4 Family:4	**V** ² ⁸ ¹¹ ² Vanadium	**25** **Cr** Chromium 51.996	**Mn** Manganese	**Fe** Iron Period:4 Family:8	**Co** ² ⁸ ¹⁵ ² Cobalt
37 **Rb** Rubidium	**Sr** Strontium 87.62	**Y** Yttrium	**Zr** ² ⁸ ¹⁸ ⁹ ² Zirconium Period:5 Family:4	**41** **Nb** Niobium	**Mo** Molybdenum 95.94	**Tc** Technetium	**Ru** ² ⁸ ¹⁸ ¹³ ² Ruthenium Period:5 Family:8	**45** **Rh** Rhodium
Cs ² ⁸ ¹⁸ ¹⁸ ¹ Cesium	**Ba** Barium Period:6 Family:2	**Hf** Hafnium Period:6 Family:4	**73** **Ta** Tantalum	**W** Tungsten 183.85	**Re** ² ⁸ ¹⁸ ³² ¹³ ² Rhenium	**Os** Osmium Period:6 Family:8	**77** **Ir** Iridium	**Pt** Platinum 195.09
Fr ² ⁸ ¹⁸ ³² ¹⁸ ⁸ ¹ Francium	**Ra** Radium Period:7 Family:2	**Rf** Rutherfordium (263) Period:7 Family:4	**105** **Db** Dubnium	**Sg** Seaborgium Period:7 Family:6	**Bh** ² ⁸ ¹⁸ ³² ¹³ ² Bohrium	**Hs** Hassium (269)	**109** **Mt** Meitnerium	

Elements Game Tiles

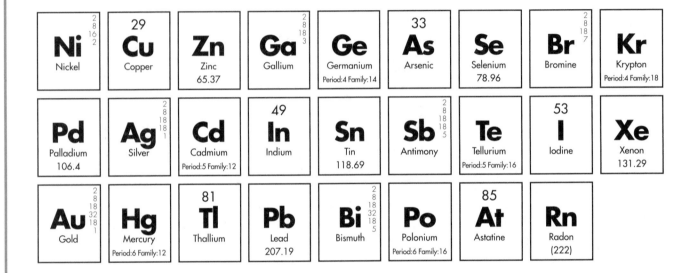

Ni 2 8 16 2 Nickel	**Cu** 29 Copper	**Zn** Zinc 65.37	**Ga** 2 8 18 3 Gallium	**Ge** Germanium Period:4 Family:14	**As** 33 Arsenic	**Se** Selenium 78.96	**Br** 2 8 18 7 Bromine	**Kr** Krypton Period:4 Family:18
Pd Palladium 106.4	**Ag** 2 8 18 18 1 Silver	**Cd** Cadmium Period:5 Family:12	**In** 49 Indium	**Sn** Tin 118.69	**Sb** 2 8 18 18 5 Antimony	**Te** Tellurium Period:5 Family:16	**I** 53 Iodine	**Xe** Xenon 131.29
Au 2 8 18 32 18 1 Gold	**Hg** Mercury Period:6 Family:12	**Tl** 81 Thallium	**Pb** Lead 207.19	**Bi** 2 8 18 32 18 5 Bismuth	**Po** Polonium Period:6 Family:16	**At** 85 Astatine	**Rn** Radon (222)	

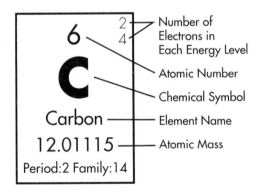

6

C

Carbon

12.01115

Period:2 Family:14

2
4 — Number of Electrons in Each Energy Level

— Atomic Number

— Chemical Symbol

— Element Name

— Atomic Mass

Simple Chemistry • EMC 878

Elements Game Tiles

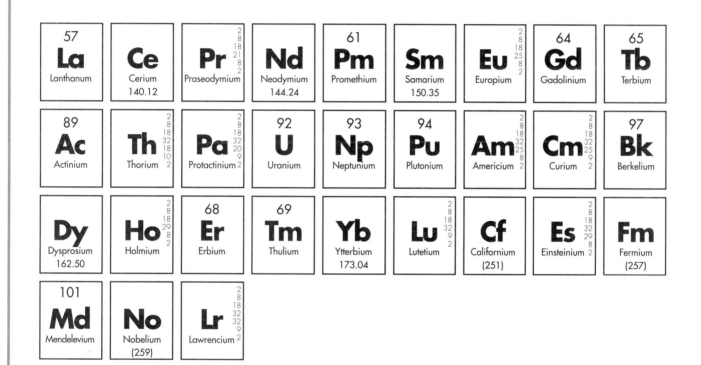

Elements Game Board

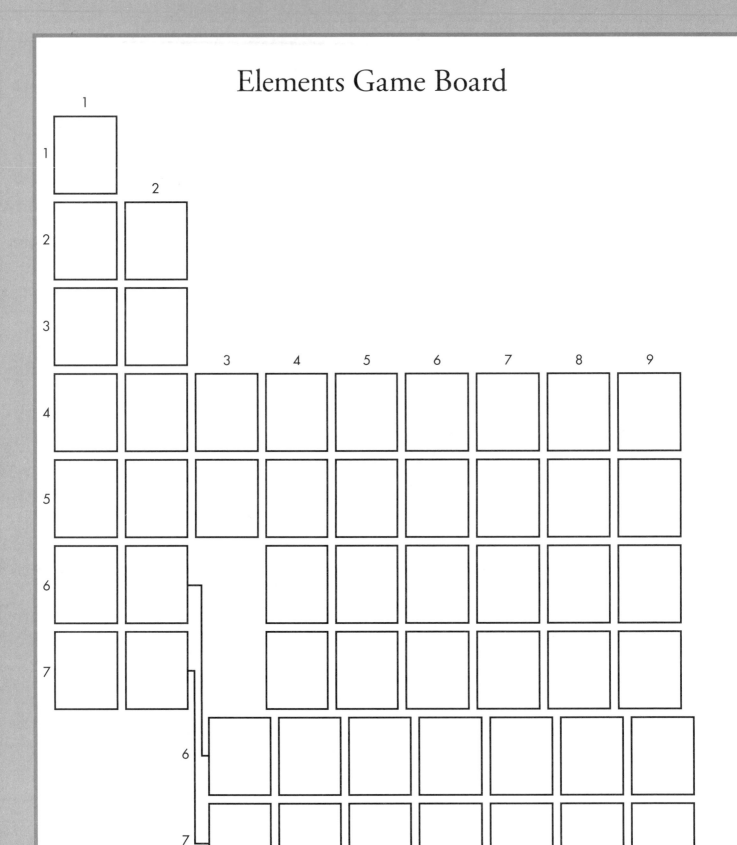

18

13 14 15 16 17

10 11 12

When substances react chemically, they can form new substances.

Prepare in Advance

Investigation 2: Make a Borax solution by dissolving 8 tablespoons (96 g) of Borax in 1 liter of hot tap water. Collect examples of common polymers, including plastic bags, plastic soda bottles, plastic wrap, styrofoam cups, latex balloons, nylon stockings, polyester clothing, chewing gum, cellulose sponge, rubber ball, and a Teflon-coated frying pan.

Investigation 3: Make a sodium hydroxide (NaOH) solution as follows: Put on goggles. Mix 50 mL of ethanol with 50 mL of water to make 100 mL of a 50% ethanol solution. Pour 25 mL of the 50% ethanol solution in a 250-mL beaker. Dissolve 5 g of sodium hydroxide pellets in the beaker of ethanol solution.

To make a saturated salt solution, dissolve table salt in 100 mL of water. Continue adding salt, stirring constantly, until no more salt dissolves.

Investigation 4: Obtain 100 mL of the following chemical solutions in a concentration of .1M: sodium bromide, sodium chloride, sodium iodide, silver nitrate, and lead nitrate. Label the bottles as follows: sodium bromide—**Br;** sodium chloride—**Cl;** sodium iodide—**I;** silver nitrate—**Ag;** and lead nitrate—**Pb.** (Supply sources: Carolina Biological or Sargent Welch)

Teacher Information

A **chemical reaction** takes place when two or more substances interact to form one or more new substances. (The decompositon of a single substance into two or more different substances is also considered a chemical reaction.) The substances that exist before a reaction takes place and that undergo a chemical change are called the **reactants.** The substances that exist after a reaction has taken place are called the **products.**

There are three main types of chemical reactions. In a **synthesis reaction,** two or more simple substances combine to form a more complex substance. In a **decomposition reaction,** a complex substance breaks down into simpler parts. **Replacement reactions** occur when the elements that make up the reactants switch places in the products.

Regardless of the type of chemical reaction, three facts remain: 1) The products of a chemical reaction will never contain elements not found in the reactants; 2) the properties of the products will be different from those of the reactants; and 3) the mass of the products will always equal the mass of the reactants.

So how do you know when a chemical reaction is taking place? Evidence can include a change in the temperature of the substances, a color change, energy released or taken in, the formation of bubbles indicating that a gas is being produced, and the formation of an insoluble solid, called a **precipitate.**

In this section, students will observe a number of chemical reactions, each of which produces a new substance: rust, a polymer similar to Slime®, soap, carbon dioxide gas, and several precipitates.

Types of Chemical Reactions

Simple substances combine to produce a complex substance.

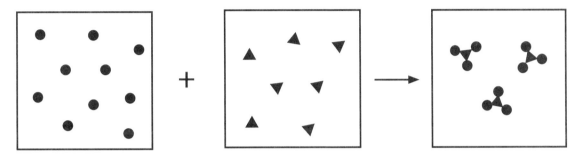

A complex substance breaks down into simpler substances.

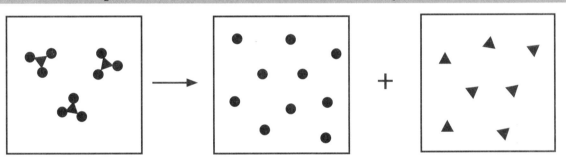

Reactants switch places in the products.

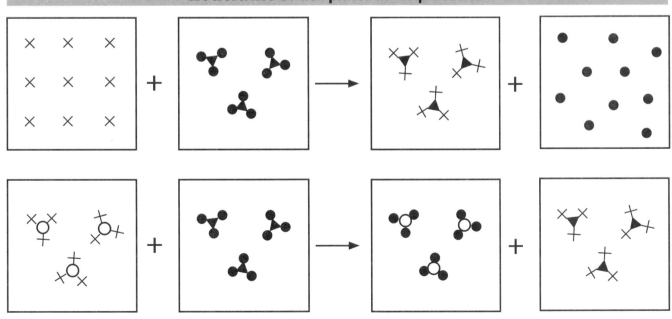

69

Concept **6** Simple Chemistry

Investigation 1

Rusting

Materials

- student record sheet on page 71, reproduced for each student
- glass jars with lids
- fine steel wool (from a hardware store)
- tap water
- markers
- masking tape
- magnifiers
- paper towels

Steps to Follow

1. Ask students if they have ever seen rust. Tell them that rust can form on objects that contain iron. In this investigation they are going to learn what causes rust to form on iron objects.

2. Divide students into small groups. Give each group two steel wool pads. Tell them that steel wool contains iron.

3. Have students wet one steel wool pad under the faucet and place it in a jar. Tell them to label the jar "Wet Steel Wool." Tell students to place a dry steel wool pad in the other jar and label it "Dry Steel Wool." Have them screw the lids on both jars.

4. Ask students to predict what will happen to the steel wool in each jar over the next two days. Have students set their jars aside and record their predictions on their record sheets.

5. Two days later, have students remove the steel wool pads from each jar, place them on a paper towel, and examine them with a magnifier. Have them record their observations.

6. Tell students that rust is evidence of a chemical reaction called **oxidation.** When iron (Fe) oxidizes, it binds with oxygen (O) atoms to form ferric oxide (Fe_2O_3), also called rust. Explain that water is an oxidizing agent (an agent is a substance that speeds up a reaction). It causes oxygen to stick to the surfaces of metal objects that contain iron and make them rust. That's why the wet steel wool rusted so fast. But dry steel wool will rust eventually too, since air usually contains at least some water vapor.

Follow-Up

Ask students what effect they think salt has on the rusting (oxidation) process. Have them pour about ½ inch (1.3 cm) of tap water in one jar and ½ inch (1.3 cm) of salty water in a second jar, and place a steel wool pad in each jar. Which steel wool pad rusts faster? (The one in salty water. Salt also speeds up the oxidation process.)

Rusting

Procedure and Observations

1. Where have you seen rust?

   _____

2. What do you think causes rust to form?

   _____

3. Place a wet steel wool pad in one jar and a dry steel wool pad in another. Label the jars and screw on the caps.

4. What do you think will happen to the wet steel wool pad over the next two days?

   _____

5. What do you think will happen to the dry steel wool pad over the next two days?

   _____

6. Let the jars sit for two days.

7. Two days later, examine each steel wool pad with a magnifier. What do you observe?

   _____

   _____

Conclusions

8. Summarize how the process of oxidation worked in this experiment.

   _____

   _____

9. Which do you think will rust faster: a car parked in the driveway or a car parked in a garage? Why?

   _____

   _____

Investigation 2

Polymers

Materials

See advance preparation on page 68.

- student record sheet on page 73, reproduced for each student
- common polymers
- bottle of white glue
- Borax solution
- 250-mL beakers
- paper cups
- self-locking plastic sandwich bags
- stirring rods
- Tbsp. measuring spoon
- pitcher
- hot tap water
- goggles

Steps to Follow

1. Divide students into small groups. Tell each group to pour 50 mL of glue into a paper cup and examine and record its properties on the chart on their record sheets.

2. Now have groups pour 50 mL of Borax solution in a paper cup and examine and record its properties on the chart.

3. Ask students to predict what will happen when the substances are mixed.

4. Tell groups to pour the glue and Borax solution into a plastic bag and seal it. Have them mix the substances by kneading the bag.

5. After the glue and Borax solution are thoroughly mixed, tell students to remove the contents of the bag and examine and record its properties on the chart.

6. Explain that they've just made a polymer, a compound made of long chains of repeating molecules (a molecule is made of two or more atoms that have bonded together). This particular polymer formed when the glue reacted chemically with the Borax solution. Polymers may be natural (rubber, cellulose, tar, shellac, tree sap) or synthetic (plastic, styrofoam, nylon, Teflon).

7. Distribute some polymers for students to examine. Ask them to list the items and their properties. (In general, polymers are dense, durable, lightweight, and strong. Many are flexible. They don't react with other substances, and make good thermal and electrical insulators.)

Follow-Up

Disposable diapers contain a polymer called sodium polyacrylate. When dry, it is a powder or crystal; when wet, it expands and turns to a gel. Sodium polyacrylate can absorb hundreds of times its weight in liquid. Have students test different brands of disposable diapers to see which is most absorbent.

Polymers

Procedure and Observations

1. Examine the glue and record its properties on the chart.

2. Examine the Borax solution and record its properties on the chart.

3. What do you think will happen when you mix these two substances together?

_____

_____

4. Mix the glue and the Borax solution in a plastic bag.

5. Remove the substance from the bag. You've just made a polymer. Record the properties of the polymer on the chart.

Substance	Properties
glue	
Borax solution	
polymer made from glue and Borax solution	

6. Examine some other examples of polymers. List the items and some of their properties.

Polymer Type	Properties

Investigation 3

Making Soap

Materials

See advance preparation on page 68.

- student record sheet on page 75, reproduced for each student
- ethanol
- sodium hydroxide (NaOH) pellets
- table salt
- saturated salt solution
- vegetable shortening
- tap water
- ice
- distilled water
- 250-mL beakers
- spoons
- graduated cylinders
- dishpan
- stirring rods
- hot plate
- balances
- cheesecloth
- goggles

Steps to Follow

1. Tell students they are going to make another useful substance by combining chemicals.

2. Divide students into small groups. Have each group place 10 g of shortening in a beaker. Tell them to slowly add 25 mL of sodium hydroxide (NaOH) solution to the beaker. (Sodium hydroxide is the chemical name for lye.)

3. Instruct students to place the beaker of shortening and NaOH solution on a hot plate and turn to medium heat. Tell students to stir until the shortening has melted and blended in completely.

4. Have them cool the mixture by placing the beaker in a dishpan of ice water.

5. After the mixture has cooled, have students stir in 50 mL of hot distilled water and 50 mL of saturated salt solution. A chemical reaction will occur to produce a substance that looks like cottage cheese soap. The salt solution makes the lye (NaOH) turn the shortening to soap.

6. Have students collect the soap by filtering it through several layers of cheesecloth. Then have students use the soap to wash their hands.

Follow-Up

Have students research the ingredients in their favorite soaps.

Making Soap

Procedure and Observations

1. Slowly add 25 mL of NaOH solution (lye) to a beaker containing 10 g of vegetable shortening.

2. Heat the substances on a hot plate. Stir until the shortening has melted.

3. Cool by placing the mixture in a dishpan of ice water.

4. Stir in 50 mL of hot distilled water and 50 mL of saturated salt solution. Describe what happens. What have you made?

   _____

   _____

   _____

   _____

5. Soap is made when lye, a fat such as shortening, and salt chemically combine. Use cheesecloth to strain the soap. Then use the soap to wash your hands.

Concept 6 — Simple Chemistry

Investigation 4

Precipitates

Materials

See advance preparation on page 68.

- student record sheet on page 77, reproduced for each student
- goggles
- small plastic cups
- sodium bromide solution
- sodium chloride solution
- sodium iodide solution
- silver nitrate solution
- lead nitrate solution
- 100 mL dropper bottles

Steps to Follow

1. Set out dropper bottles of the following solutions: sodium bromide (labeled **Br**), sodium chloride (**Cl**), sodium iodide (**I**), silver nitrate (**Ag**), and lead nitrate (**Pb**). Tell students they are going to see how these chemicals react with one another.

2. Divide the class into small groups. Have each group set up their plastic cups in two rows of three cups each.

3. Instruct students to place drops of the chemicals in each cup, as indicated below and on the diagram on their record sheet.

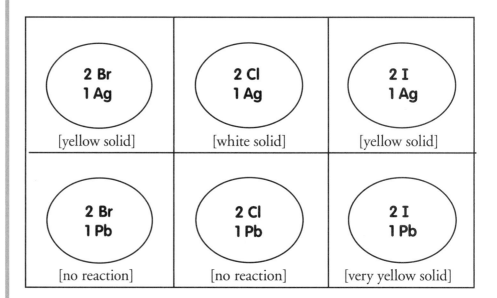

2 Br 1 Ag	2 Cl 1 Ag	2 I 1 Ag
[yellow solid]	[white solid]	[yellow solid]
2 Br 1 Pb	2 Cl 1 Pb	2 I 1 Pb
[no reaction]	[no reaction]	[very yellow solid]

4. Have students observe what happens in each cup and record their observations in the corresponding circle on the diagram.

5. Introduce the term **precipitate:** an insoluble solid that forms when a chemical reaction takes place. Ask students which combinations of chemicals underwent a chemical reaction (Br + Ag, Cl + Ag, I + Ag, I + Pb).

Follow-Up

Challenge students to separate out the precipitates using filter paper. Tell them to allow the substances to dry overnight and examine them the next day. How is each precipitate different from the chemicals that made it?

Name ____________________________________

Concept 6 Simple Chemistry

Investigation 4

Precipitates

Procedure and Observations

1. Arrange your cups in two rows of three cups each.
2. Place drops of chemicals in each cup, according to the diagram below. For example, the cup in the upper left gets two drops of sodium bromide (Br) and one drop of silver nitrate (Ag).
3. Record your observations in the corresponding circle.

	2 drops Br	2 drops Cl	2 drops I
1 drop Ag			
1 drop Pb			

Conclusions

4. A precipitate is evidence that a chemical reaction has taken place. Which combinations of chemicals underwent a chemical reaction? How do you know?

____

____

____

____

5. Name a precipitate produced in a previous investigation.

____

Investigation 5

Gas It Up

Materials

- student record sheet on page 79, reproduced for each student
- 16-oz. (480-mL) plastic soda bottles
- balloons
- funnels
- baking soda (sodium bicarbonate)
- vinegar
- tsp. measuring spoon

Steps to Follow

1. So far students have observed the formation of solids from chemical reactions: rust, a polymer, soap, and several unnamed precipitates. Tell students that a solid isn't the only substance that can be produced by a chemical reaction.

2. Divide students into small groups. Have each group pour 50 mL of vinegar into a 16-oz. (480-mL) plastic soda bottle.

3. Then have groups use a small funnel to pour 2 teaspoons (8 g) of baking soda into a balloon.

4. Tell students to attach the balloon securely to the mouth of the bottle, being careful not to spill any baking soda into the bottle yet. Ask students what they think will happen when the baking soda is added to the vinegar. Have them record their predictions on their record sheets.

5. Tell students to empty the baking soda from the balloon into the bottle. Have them observe and record what happens.

6. Explain that when baking soda is added to vinegar, a chemical reaction takes place and carbon dioxide (CO_2) gas is produced. The gas inflates the balloon.

Follow-Up

Repeat the activity, this time using lemon juice instead of vinegar. Then use chalk powder instead of baking soda. Each time, carbon dioxide gas is produced.

You can also add 1 teaspoon (4 g) of dry yeast to 20 mL of hydrogen peroxide. The gas produced this time is oxygen.

Name _____

Gas It Up

Procedure and Observations

1. Pour 50 mL of vinegar in a soda bottle.

2. Use a funnel to pour 8 g of baking soda into a balloon.

3. Attach the balloon to the mouth of the bottle. Be careful not to spill any baking soda in the bottle yet.

4. What do you think will happen when the baking soda is added to the vinegar?

   _____

   _____

   _____

   _____

5. Empty the balloon full of baking soda into the bottle. What happens?

   _____

   _____

   _____

Conclusion

6. What is produced by this chemical reaction? What evidence do you have?

   _____

   _____

   _____